NO WAY!

Jolting Jumps

Wendy Conklin, M.A.

Consultants

Timothy Rasinski, Ph.D.
Kent State University

Lori Oczkus, M.A.
Literacy Consultant

Publishing Credits

Rachelle Cracchiolo, M.S.Ed., *Publisher*

Conni Medina, M.A.Ed., *Managing Editor*

Dona Herweck Rice, *Series Developer*

Emily R. Smith, M.A.Ed., *Content Director*

Stephanie Bernard/Susan Daddis, M.A.Ed. *Editors*

Robin Erickson, *Senior Graphic Designer*

The TIME logo is a registered trademark of TIME Inc. Used under license.

Image Credits: p.2 Muslianshah Masrie/Shutterstock.com; p.5 Dennis Hallinan/Alamy Stock Photo; p.6 Darminladiro/Shutterstock.com; p.8 ben bryant/Shutterstock.com; p.9 DeAgostini/Getty Images; pp.16–17 Vadzim Kandratsenkau/Alamy Stock Photo; p.19 Photo by Simon Ward/REX (217221b) A PARACHUTE STACK SKYDIVING-1993; p.20 blickwinkel/Alamy Stock Photo; pp.24–25, 34–35 Illustrations by Timothy J. Bradley; pp.28–29 Dean Treml/Red Bull via Getty Images; p.31 blickwinkel/Alamy Stock Photo; p.38 Bondariev Volodymyr/Dreamstime.com; all other images from iStock and/or Shutterstock.

Teacher Created Materials

5301 Oceanus Drive
Huntington Beach, CA 92649-1030
http://www.tcmpub.com
ISBN 978-1-4938-3610-9

Table of Contents

Risky Business

Have you ever dreamed of being a superhero who could fly through the air? How about soaring like an eagle with Earth beneath you? Or maybe you've thought it would be cool to surf the air after jumping out of a plane. Believe it or not, people perform these risky acts every day and live to tell about it.

The Influence of Inventions

Extreme air sports are possible because of earlier inventions. For example, skydiving and skysurfing can be done because the airplane was invented, and the invention of the parachute makes B.A.S.E. jumping and paragliding possible.

Dreaming of Flying

More than 500 years ago, Leonardo da Vinci dreamed of human flight. He sketched ideas for wings that would help humans fly, as well as a balloon that inflated in the sky. The technology did not exist in da Vinci's time for these things to become realities, but that did not stop him from dreaming about them.

Whether it's bungee jumping, skydiving, or wingsuit flying, these activities require an abundance of creativity and courage. Enthusiasts are always challenging themselves to perform better for competitions or simply to try stunts that are more difficult than anything they've done before. They spend many hours and lots of money perfecting their skills. It takes dedication to master these extreme sports.

Jumping Off a Base

You count down—three, two, one—and calmly plunge from the cliff's edge. You free fall for mere seconds before **deploying** a parachute and landing safely on the ground. Jumping from airplanes is not adventurous enough for people like you! Instead, you jump 3,212 feet (979 meters) from Angel Falls in Venezuela. For another jump, you climb an antenna tower that looms 2,000 feet (609 meters) in the air. Tall buildings that rise 1,000 feet (305 meters) provide you the thrill of a lifetime.

This extreme sport is known as *B.A.S.E. jumping*. *B.A.S.E.* is an acronym for building, antenna, span, and earth. These are the structures used as bases for the jumps. A jumper's goal is to complete jumps in all four categories and take his or her place among a group of elite jumpers.

Human Terminal Velocity

Human terminal velocity is the fastest speed a human can go while in free fall. The speed of the fall is about 120 miles per hour (mph) or about 193 kilometers per hour (kph). It takes about 12 seconds to reach this speed if the jumper falls from a height of about 1,500 feet (457 meters).

How Fast Is That?

In short jumps, jumpers often don't reach the human terminal velocity before they must deploy their chutes. After three seconds, a jumper reaches 50% of human terminal velocity. How fast, then, is that jumper traveling in mph and kph?

Buildings, Antennas, Spans, and Earth

Once a B.A.S.E. jumper completes at least one jump in all four categories, he or she is assigned a number. This number indicates the order of the jumpers who have completed the categories. The first person to do this was Phil Smith in 1981, so he will forever have the B.A.S.E. number of 1. This is known as a *forever number*.

B

656 feet

Most buildings and monuments are locked and under surveillance. For that reason, many jumpers select buildings under construction instead. The jump from Marina Bay Sands in Singapore is a favorite at 656 feet (200 meters).

Antenna towers are popular structures to jump from because they are often very tall and easily accessible. These jumps are usually about 1,000 feet (305 meters).

A

1,000 feet

S 876 feet

Spans or bridges must cross over large gorges or canyons to be tall enough for a jump. In Fayetteville, West Virginia, the New River Gorge Bridge is open to B.A.S.E. jumpers only one day a year, on Bridge Day. The jump is 876 feet (267 meters).

Earth includes any natural formations such as **fjords**, cliffs, and canyons. Preacher's Pulpit in Lysefjord, Norway, is a 1,982-foot (604-meter) drop and is a popular place for B.A.S.E. jumping.

E 1,982 feet

Pilot Chutes

Some B.A.S.E. jumpers use **pilot chutes**. These are larger chutes than ones used in skydiving because the jumps are made from lower **altitudes** and speeds. The pilot chute opens and creates an initial drag before the main chute opens. This method helps increase the safety of the sport, since most B.A.S.E. jumpers don't pack a backup chute.

B.A.S.E. jumping is the most risky of all jumping sports because the jumps are so close to the ground. These short distances leave very little time to deploy parachutes before reaching the ground. If a jumper is not quick enough releasing a chute, the fall could be deadly. In preparation for B.A.S.E. jumping, it is recommended that a person completes at least 100 skydives. During a skydive, the jumper has more time to become familiar with parachute gear. If the chute doesn't deploy right away, the jumper has time to redeploy the chute or use a backup chute. B.A.S.E. jumpers are not so lucky.

How Far Will You Fall?

If you free fall 164 feet per second, how far will you have fallen after 7 seconds?

The distance of a free fall on a B.A.S.E. jump usually determines how the jumpers will hold their chutes. Jumpers can hold chutes in their hands or in backpack pockets. A short jump only allows about two seconds of free fall before jumpers have to deploy their chutes. For very short distances, most jumpers use handheld chutes. At 250 feet (76 meters) from the ground, a handheld chute is easier and quicker to deploy. Longer jumps allow about seven seconds of free fall, so jumpers have more time to deploy their chutes.

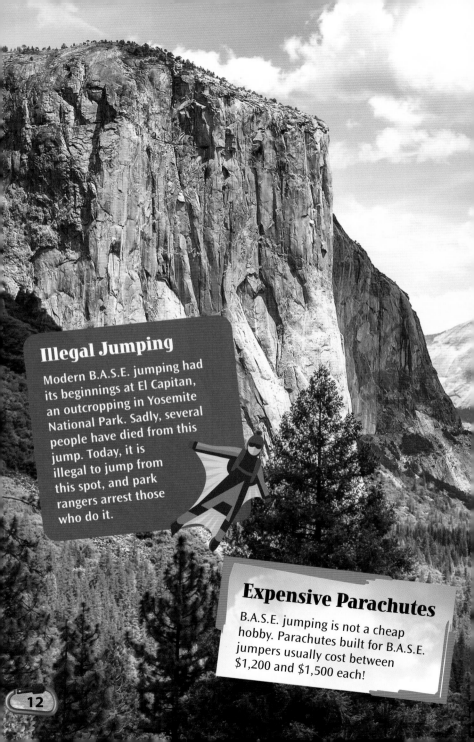

Illegal Jumping

Modern B.A.S.E. jumping had its beginnings at El Capitan, an outcropping in Yosemite National Park. Sadly, several people have died from this jump. Today, it is illegal to jump from this spot, and park rangers arrest those who do it.

Expensive Parachutes

B.A.S.E. jumping is not a cheap hobby. Parachutes built for B.A.S.E. jumpers usually cost between $1,200 and $1,500 each!

B.A.S.E. jumps require a certain kind of parachute or canopy. A **ram-air canopy** is among the most popular because it deploys quickly and gives the jumper steering control. If jumping off an outcrop, a jumper needs to steer clear of jagged rocks. A **round canopy**, by comparison, doesn't provide as much steering control.

The most important skill for B.A.S.E. jumpers is the ability to judge whether to jump. This decision needs to be made carefully. Jumpers consider the wind, the surrounding structures, and the landing site. Besides making the jump, it is just as important that B.A.S.E. jumpers take on the ritual of hiking to the top of the structure, known as the **exit point**. This ritual gives jumpers time to plan the different parts of their jumps. There is very little time during jumps, so jumpers must visualize their plans beforehand. They see in their minds how the jump will go, step by step.

Since B.A.S.E. jumping is so risky, it has become illegal in many places. Although some jumpers break the law, most B.A.S.E. jumpers defy gravity by safely following rules and regulations.

Oh, Go Jump Out of an Airplane!

The plane climbs higher and higher until it reaches 13,000 feet (3,962 meters). Going any higher than 15,000 feet (4,572 meters) would require supplemental oxygen to breathe. When the plane flies over the drop zone, you jump out. You free fall for 60 seconds before throwing out your pilot chute, which deploys your parachute. You steer the chute toward the target and land safely.

Skydiving Methods

Skydiving students learn to skydive using one or more methods. For the static-line method, the parachute automatically deploys once the jumper is out of the way of the aircraft. There is very little free-fall time in this method. For the tandem free-fall method, the jumper is connected to a certified instructor during the fall. For the accelerated free-fall method, a student jumps solo. But to be safe, the instructor jumps near the student until the parachute deploys.

You Have a Backup!

Parachutes have automatic activation devices (AAD) in case jumpers become unconscious or lose track of when to deploy the parachutes. An AAD is a tiny computer that keeps track of the altitude and will deploy a reserve chute if necessary.

The Mass of the Skydivers

In a normal skydive, a person's mass causes him or her to free fall at the rate of 120 mph (193 kph). But in a tandem fall, the combined mass causes the person and the instructor to free fall at 200 mph. What is the percent increase in the free-fall rates between the two jumps?

Parachuting Pilot

Cheryl Stearns is a pilot and one of the most accomplished skydivers in the world. She made her first jump at the age of 17. In 1977, she joined the U.S. Army and became the first female of the elite Army Golden Knights parachute team. After her time in the Army, she went on to win several parachuting and accuracy awards.

This young woman is packing a parachute.

Controlling the Chute

The most important piece of equipment for a skydiver is the parachute. If a chute does not deploy correctly, the skydiver's life is in danger. It's best not to have surprises while free falling 13,000 feet (3,962 meters) in the air! Packing the chute the same way every time is important so that it always opens safely. Not packing it correctly could result in twisted lines or quick deployment, which could hurt the jumper or damage the equipment.

To control the landing, skydivers use ram-air parachutes. Ram-air chutes contain two sets of lines, one on the right side and one on the left side of the chute, each set connected to **toggles**. When a jumper pulls on the lines on the right, the chute lowers on that side. This **decelerates** and turns the jumper to the right. The same thing happens on the left side when a jumper pulls down on the left lines. If a jumper wants to slow down the fall, he or she pulls on the lines on both sides.

Parachute Fabric

Parachutes are made using a **zero porosity** fabric with a special coating that does not allow air to flow through the fabric. This gives jumpers the best performance possible from the parachutes. However, it can also make it difficult to get all the air out when folding the parachutes!

Skydiving Tricks

It takes practice to learn how to jump from an airplane. Once a jumper feels more comfortable jumping from an airplane, he or she can work on more advanced tricks. Some of these tricks help in skydiving competitions. These competitions include target accuracy, formation free fall, and canopy stacking.

Landing on a target that is just 20 inches (50.8 centimeters) in diameter takes a lot of skill. In 2014, Elena Borisova, a female skydiver from Kazakhstan, won a competition in accuracy at an event in Russia. Not only did she come in first place in the female division, but she also defeated the men.

Formation free fall is when several skydivers jump together. As they fall, they hold on to one another to create a formation. In 2006, skydivers in Thailand created a 400-diver formation, establishing a new world record.

Canopy-stacking formation happens once jumpers deploy their parachutes. One by one, the jumpers form a vertical line. They do this by hooking their feet into the lines of the canopy of the jumper below. The goal is for all the jumpers to stack their canopies one on top of the other. In 2007, 100 jumpers set a world record when they created a stacked canopy formation.

Ballet Diving

One competitive skydiving sport is aerial ballet. The jumper performs gymnastic movements in the sky. These are captured on video and then judged.

STOP! THINK...

Four skydivers landed at these coordinates on a map. Which skydiver landed closest to the target, which is at the origin or bull's-eye?

- Randy (7, –9)
- Maria (8, 7)
- Ty (–5, 9)
- Reagan (–8, –1)

Surfing the Sky

You strap the board to your feet and leap from an airplane that is 10,000 feet (3,048 meters) above the ground. You stand on the board, leaning into the wind and surfing across the sky. With this board, you have greater **lateral** movement than if you were simply skydiving. Your board creates drag, but you manage to control it with your strength. You easily change directions and perform rolls, helicopter spins, and loops. You have mastered the art of skysurfing.

Not just anyone can skysurf; only very experienced skydivers have the ability to control the boards strapped to their feet while free falling at more than 120 mph (193 kph). Most skysurfers use boards shaped like snowboards and wear parachutes so they can land safely. If a skysurfer loses control, he or she can cut away the bindings on the board and gain control. Just as in skydiving, the parachute deploys and the skysurfer lands without harm. Today, many skysurfers compete while a free-falling cameraman captures their stunts.

Skysurf Slang

Skysurfers have their own slang terms for the sport. For example, *chicken soup* refers to a jump that doesn't go as well as planned. To *helicopter* is to spin your body to make the board look like chopper blades.

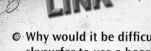

- Why would it be difficult for a skysurfer to use a board the size of a surfboard?

- Why would a set of skis present problems for a skysurfer rather than a snowboard?

- What kinds of challenges would a skydiving cameraman have while trying to film a skysurfer?

Glide Like an Eagle

With just a few brisk steps, you launch your hang glider off the hill into the sky and soar like an eagle. You glide through the crisp air with your wings above and Earth thousands of feet below. Instead of falling to Earth, you find **thermals** that allow you to rise higher and higher, even above the birds. **Updrafts** of air keep you flying for hours, but at some point, the thermals diminish. You gently glide down to land and touch the ground. You are hooked on the ability to fly.

There are two types of gliding: hang gliding and paragliding. Both involve using air currents and a pilot's foot speed for taking off. There are two important differences between hang gliders and paragliders. Hang gliders are rigid and have metal frames, and the glider maintains a horizontal position during flight. A paraglider uses a ram-air canopy and glides in a seated position.

The hang gliding wing came about in the 1960s, thanks to the work of NASA engineer Francis Rogallo. While researching parachutes and kites as a way for spacecrafts to land back on Earth, he invented the **delta wing parachute**. A few other individuals took this lightweight structure and perfected it into the hang gliding wing that is most often used by professionals today.

A hang glider takes off.

Paragliding

Paragliding is a free-flying sport that uses a wide canopy, similar to a parachute, to suspend a person in air. The canopy is attached to the pilot's body by a harness, which doubles as a seat. The canopy is deployed before the pilot runs to gain **momentum** and jumps off a cliff. The canopy inflates with air, and the pilot takes off!

Gliders' Gear and Guidance

There are two different types of hang gliders: the *flex wing* and the *rigid wing*. The flex-wing glider is made of cables and **battens** that create a curved wing shape. Air flows over the curved surface, allowing the wing to lift. Rigid-wing gliders are composed of fiberglass and tend to be much heavier than flex wings. However, they also perform better for the pilot.

To be safe, the pilot wears a helmet, goggles, and a parachute. He attaches himself to the glider with a harness. To launch a hang glider, a pilot runs down an incline to generate air movement of about 15 to 25 mph (24 to 40 kph). During this short run, the air glides over the top of the wing, lift occurs, and the glider takes off from the ground. The combined weight of the glider and the pilot keeps the glider from going too far up into the sky and keeps the air flowing over the wings, propelling the glider forward. The pilot gets lift from thermals or from ridge lifts in which air bounces off mountain ridges or cliffs. The pilot can also get wave lift, which is created when winds pass over a mountain on the **leeward** side.

thermal lift

wind direction

24

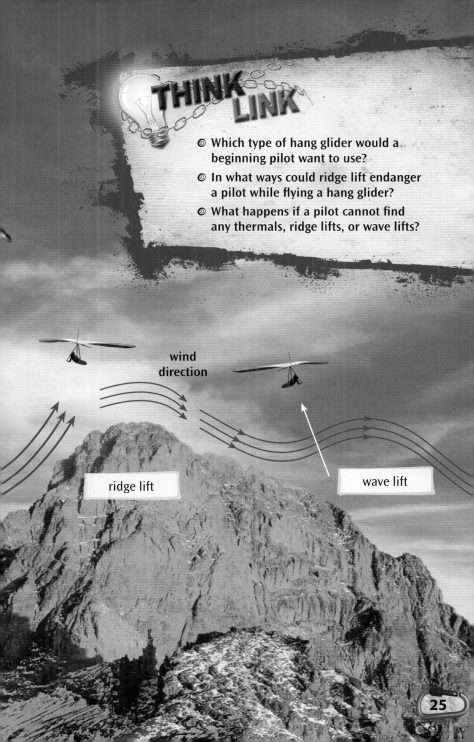

THINK LINK

- Which type of hang glider would a beginning pilot want to use?
- In what ways could ridge lift endanger a pilot while flying a hang glider?
- What happens if a pilot cannot find any thermals, ridge lifts, or wave lifts?

wind direction

ridge lift

wave lift

A hang-glider pilot gets information about a flight through an altimeter, which tells the altitude, and a variometer, which tells how fast the glider is climbing or descending. If the hang glider reaches a really high altitude, the pilot will need an oxygen mask. Lack of oxygen could make the pilot sick or impair his or her judgment.

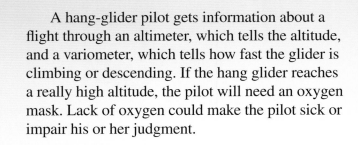

How Many Miles?

If a hang glider travels for 11 hours at the speed of 43 mph, how many miles will it travel?

A pilot controls his or her flight using the **control bar** and his or her body. A pilot shifts his or her body to control the direction of the glider. He or she can pull back on the control bar and tip the nose down or push forward and tip the nose up. By tipping the nose of the glider down, the pilot causes the glider to speed up. By tipping the nose up, the glider slows down and can even stall in midair. A pilot can make a safe landing on his or her feet by slowing down the hang glider.

High and Long

Some hang gliders fly at 18,000 feet (5,486 meters), higher than many birds. These flights can last several hours. In fact, the longest glider flight on record is 11 hours in the air.

Diving Off a Cliff

You look down to the water below. You're on a cliff that's 85 feet (26 meters) high, as tall as an eight-story building! You calm your nerves by focusing your mind on the dive zone. No special equipment is necessary for this sport, just your body. As with any extreme sport, helmets are recommended. There are only three seconds to perform two somersaults in the air before hitting the water. You rise on your toes and dive. Your stunts are perfect, and you enter the water feet first, scoring a perfect 10 points. As a professional cliff diver, this is not your first diving competition.

Birdman

Cliff diving dates back to 1770, when the last king of Maui dove off a cliff 63 feet (19 meters) high without making a splash. He earned the name Birdman and demanded that his warriors prove their loyalty and courage by diving off cliffs, too.

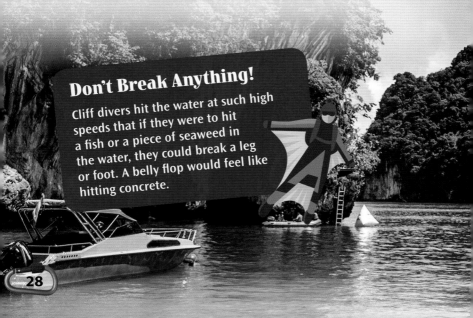

Don't Break Anything!

Cliff divers hit the water at such high speeds that if they were to hit a fish or a piece of seaweed in the water, they could break a leg or foot. A belly flop would feel like hitting concrete.

Height Relates to Speed

When you jump off a cliff, you travel at 9.8 meters per second. Gravity pulls you toward the water. How long will it take a cliff diver to hit the water if she jumps from 20 meters? How about from 30 meters? What about from 3 meters?

A professional cliff diver's goal is to enter the water with as little splash as possible. A diver will straighten his body, keep his arms to his sides, press his feet together, and point his toes. Entering the water feet first ensures that the diver will touch as little of the water's surface area as possible.

Most dives are from heights ranging from 80 to 115 feet (24 to 35 meters). The force of gravity pulls cliff divers toward the water. Known as **free-fall acceleration**, this rate means that the longer the dive, the faster the diver travels through air toward the water. This happens because the diver has more time to accelerate during the dive.

The height of the fall dictates how fast the diver enters the water. Once the diver hits the water, the speed decreases to almost zero. Traveling at high speeds creates stress on the diver's body and can lead to injuries or death.

Showing Off

Cliff divers who perform shows can dive from up to 148 feet (45 meters). These divers have a lot of experience. However, sometimes injuries do occur even with experienced divers.

Superheroes in the Sky

You climb to the tallest **precipice**, dive head first, spread your wingsuit, and fly. The wingsuit, which looks like a snow angel or a flying squirrel, allows you to soar horizontally through the air at high speeds, much like a superhero, until you deploy your parachute and land safely. For a brief moment, you do feel like a superhero with the power to fly! You can't wait to experience your next wingsuit dive.

Wingsuits

When a wingsuit diver jumps from a tall building or a moving plane, both weight and gravity pull the diver toward the ground. The wingsuit provides lift to propel the diver through the air as she descends toward Earth. Wingsuits have webbed surfaces that fill with air under the arms and between the legs. The suit acts like a large wing as the force of air opens the membranes in the suit. The diver then uses her body to control her movements in the sky.

Which Is More Thrilling?

A wingsuit diver soars across the sky at 70 mph, while a skydiver travels 30 mph horizontally through the air. A wingsuit flyer falls at a rate of 50 mph, while a skydiver falls at a rate of 120 mph. Who would cover more distance in a given elapsed time, the wingsuit flyer or skydiver?

They Cost *How* Much?!

Wingsuits are handmade, which can hike up their prices. The cost of a wingsuit starts at around $1,000. But more experienced flyers often buy suits that cost twice that amount!

Steering a Wingsuit

After jumping, straighten your legs and your spine while spreading the wings on your arms and legs. This will help you to gain surface area. Increased surface area helps produce the lift necessary for flying.

If the goal is to go a long distance, get into a head-low position.

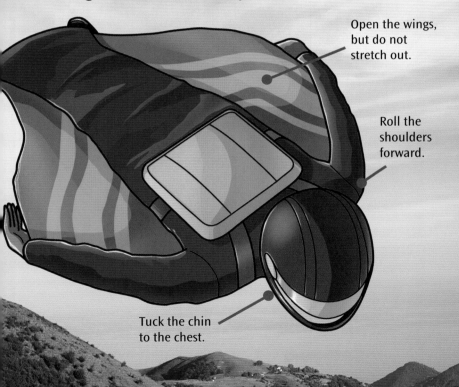

Open the wings, but do not stretch out.

Roll the shoulders forward.

Tuck the chin to the chest.

If the aim is more flying time, get into a head-up position.

Stretch the wings as much as possible to gain maximum surface area.

Raise the head so that it is looking forward.

To turn, make small movements by twisting the shoulders, hips, legs, and feet.

Jump, Bounce, and Roll!

You stand with your ankles tethered to bungee cords. You take the plunge and swan dive off a platform that is 200 feet (61 meters) aboveground. The ground seems to rush toward you until you feel a quick snap and a jolt that keeps you from crashing. You bounce back up and down until the momentum eases, and you hang upside down. As a bungee-jumping junkie, you love the rush of **adrenaline** this sport gives you.

The Legend Behind Bungee Jumping

Legend says that bungee jumping began at Pentecost Island in the South Pacific, when a woman wanted to escape her husband who she felt was mistreating her. She climbed a tall tree, and as her husband began to follow her, she tied a vine to her ankles. Just as he reached out to grab her, she jumped. He fell to his death, while she bounced back. The men of the village began imitating this stunt to see how she did it. Over the years, villagers began jumping from a tower on the island. It wasn't until the 1970s that a Westerner brought this bungee jumping phenomenon across the ocean.

Not Just Jumping Rope!

A new sport called *rope jumping* is similar to bungee jumping except that jumpers dive off a platform with nylon ropes that do not stretch.

In spite of how dangerous bungee jumping seems, most people consider this to be the safest of the extreme sports. Jumpers wear helmets and safety harnesses, and in some jumps, they wear two harnesses. The stretchy cord wraps around the ankles of the jumper.

The intensity of the jump is dependent on the weight of the jumper, the distance of the jump, and the stretch of the cords. Once the person jumps, the energy builds and stores in the cord until the cord stretches to its farthest point. Then, the **potential energy** stored in the cord releases and propels the jumper back up for a few more free falls until the cord comes to a stop. While most people jump with longer cords to allow for longer free falls and greater deceleration once the cord catches, heavier people jump with shorter cords. The shorter cords catch the free fall earlier and make the jump more comfortable.

Shock Cords for More Weight

Shock cords are added to the bungee cord to accommodate weight. One cord is used for every 23 kg. How many shock cords would need to be added for a jumper weighing 100 kg?

Zorbing Fun!

Have you ever wondered what it's like to be a sock in a washing machine? If you ride in a zorb filled with five gallons of water, you would know! A zorb is a large ball made from two layers of plastic material. The ball rolls downhill on a track. To protect and cushion a rider, there is about 459 cubic feet (13 cubic meters) of air and a harness that straps the rider into the middle of the zorb.

Going at Zorb Speed

The speed of a zorb ride depends on the weight of the rider, the headwind, and whether a rider is strapped in. Riders who are strapped in cause the zorb to roll faster.

At the top of the hill, a zorb operator pushes the ball so that it begins rolling down a track, typically 700 feet (213 meters) long. The zorb gains speed and momentum. It might seem that rolling around and around inside a ball would make a rider sick. But the zorb is so large that it takes 30 feet (9 meters) for a rider to complete a full rotation inside the ball. Therefore, a rider isn't spinning too fast. Once the zorb reaches the bottom of the hill, it comes to a stop, and the ride is over.

Zorb Circumference

If it takes 30 feet to complete a full rotation of the zorb, about what length is the diameter of the zorb?

Take It to the Limit

What would entice a person to jump off a building, step out of a plane, or dive off a cliff? Is it the desire for an adrenaline rush? Is it a craving for a brush with danger? People who participate in these extreme sports feel that it's more than that. The people in this select group love what they do.

Risk-takers spend time training and preparing for the things most people consider dangerous. They test their limits and push the boundaries of what is possible. But they perform under conditions that are relatively safe because of their familiarity with the sport and the care they take in preparing and building their skills. Whether it is hang gliding, bungee jumping, or rolling down a hill inside a ball, these individuals love the challenge and excitement of free-falling sports. They'll do whatever they need to do to take that leap and jump!

Always Start at the Beginning

To be safe, all free-fall activities require people to start at the easiest level so that they can learn the skills first. Once they master the small skills, it's possible to go to the next level and try something harder.

Glossary

adrenaline—a hormone released when frightened, excited, or angered that speeds up heart rate and increases blood flow

altitudes—heights of objects above sea level

battens—thin strips of wood inserted into glider wings

control bar—bar that a pilot of a hang glider holds on to and controls his or her glider

decelerates—reduces speed

delta wing parachute—a type of parachute used in hang gliding

deploying—opening a parachute while free-falling

exit point—the top of the structure that a B.A.S.E. jumper jumps from

fjords—narrow inlets of the sea between cliffs or steep slopes

free-fall acceleration—the idea that a person continues to accelerate in a fall because of the force of gravity

lateral—across, horizontally

leeward—downwind; located on the side of a mountain sheltered from the wind.

momentum—the act of gaining speed, forward motion, and active force

pilot chutes—smaller chutes that help anchor jumpers and open main parachutes

potential energy—stored energy

precipice—a tall, dangerous peak or cliff

ram-air canopy—a square or rectangular parachute with two nylon layers that fill with air, making control easier

round canopy—dome-shaped parachute

thermals—hot columns of air

toggles—the pulls on a ram-air parachute that control and slow the chute

updrafts—warm air currents moving upward

zero porosity—a characteristic of a specialized fabric through which no air can pass

Index

Check It Out!

Books

Clark, Tracy. 2016. *Mirage*. HMH Books for Young Readers.

Higgins, Matt. 2014. *Bird Dream: Adventures at the Extremes of Human Flight*. Penguin Press.

Kalman, Bobbie, and John Crossingham. 2006. *Extreme Skydiving*. Crabtree Publishing Company.

Lewis, Wendy A. 2008. *Freefall*. Key Porter Books.

Tomlinson, Joe. 2004. *Extreme Sports: In Search of the Ultimate Thrill*. Firefly Books.

Zeigler, Heidi. 2003. *Hang Gliding*. Rosen Book Works, Inc.

Videos

Roede, Christian, Eric Ellioth, Preben Hansen, and Thomas O. Christensen. 2015. *Wingmen*. Xtreme Video.

Strauch, Marah. 2015. *Sunshine Superman*. Magnolia Pictures.

VanderMost, Macaela. 2012. *Sky High*. Kinonation.

Try It!

Design an exhibit for the National Smithsonian Air and Space Museum chronicling the advancements of individual human flight. Your display has room to feature five different advancements in technology.

- ◎ Which technologies from the book will you choose to feature?

- ◎ How will they be displayed? Chronologically? Based on importance?

- ◎ What statistics about human flight will you include in your display?

- ◎ What true stories about human flight will you tell?

About the Author

Besides writing books for students and conducting training sessions for teachers, Wendy Conklin has a wide variety of interests, from reviving old furniture to competing in rigorous athletic competitions. If there's a challenge, she jumps right in to take it on. Her motto in life is to live life to the fullest and have no regrets. Someday, Wendy hopes to live in Hawaii, but right now, she lives with her family and two sweet Boston terriers in Round Rock, Texas.

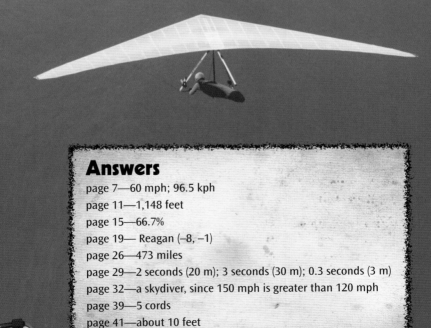

Answers
page 7—60 mph; 96.5 kph
page 11—1,148 feet
page 15—66.7%
page 19— Reagan (–8, –1)
page 26—473 miles
page 29—2 seconds (20 m); 3 seconds (30 m); 0.3 seconds (3 m)
page 32—a skydiver, since 150 mph is greater than 120 mph
page 39—5 cords
page 41—about 10 feet